SPIRIT OF

THE KEIGHLEY
AND WORTH
VALLEY RAILWAY

MIKE HEATH

First published in Great Britain in 2010

Copyright text and photographs © 2010 Mike Heath

British Library Cataloguing-in-Publication Data
A CIP record for this title is available from the British Library

ISBN 978 1 906887 80 3

PiXZ Books
Halsgrove House, Ryelands Industrial Estate,
Bagley Road, Wellington, Somerset TA21 9PZ
Tel: 01823 653777
Fax: 01823 216796
email: sales@halsgrove.com

An imprint of Halstar Ltd, part of the Halsgrove group of companies
Information on all Halsgrove titles is available at: www.halsgrove.com

Printed and bound in China by Toppan Leefung Printing Ltd

Introduction

The Keighley and Worth Valley Railway, which was originally opened in 1865, spent much of its first 100 years of existence known only to the West Yorkshire community it was built to serve. Then, during the swinging '60s, branch lines all over the country were closed as part of British Rail's streamlining policy which also saw the replacement of steam locomotives with diesel and electric traction.

The Worth Valley line itself was closed in 1962 but local people teamed up with railway enthusiasts in an effort to save it. Their determination saw the setting up of a preservation society which was the first to purchase a standard gauge railway from BR. Many years of volunteer toil resulted in the line reopening on 29 June 1968 since when the railway has been managed and operated by qualified volunteers who have now provided services for over four decades and justifiably celebrated forty years of operation in 2008.

The Keighley and Worth Valley Railway Preservation Society is rightly proud of having preserved the branch line in its entirety and the decision to recreate and maintain the superb late 1950s' – early 1960s' house style found along the line.

What follows is a photographic journey along the route which starts alongside the BR station at Keighley and climbs through the diverse West Yorkshire landscape to the line's terminus at Oxenhope, highlighting the magnificent Brontë countryside and the effect that the changing seasons and weather have on it. Stepping back in time at each of the beautifully restored stations at Ingrow, Damems, Oakworth and Haworth along the way, and celebrating the many and varied events that the railway holds creating a 'Worth Valley Experience' enjoyed by thousands of visitors each year.

TRAIN SERVICES

TO HAWORTH & OXENHOPE

TIME	PLAT FORM	TIME	PLAT FORM

SPECIAL NOTICES

Take a
DRIVERS EYE VIEW
of the line.

Ask for a
DAY ROVER
TICKET

TICKETS
AND
ENQUIRIES

Left:
The ramped approach to the platforms at Keighley. On the right is the ticket office, a tobacco kiosk rescued from Manchester's old Central Station. To the left is the ticket collectors hut, formerly a telephone box at Wakefield Kirkgate Station.

Passenger trains usually depart from platform 4 which retains many original features such as the splendid glass canopy with its ornate cast iron supports.

5

On Steam Gala days vintage shuttles run from platform 3. In 2008 the railway celebrated its 40th anniversary and the Vintage Carriages Trust's locomotive 'Sir Berkeley' which dates from 1891 returned to the line to haul some of the these trains. For the event an ex-Metropolitan coach had been repainted in the blue and cream livery carried for the re-opening train back in 1968.

On the evening of another gala the vintage train was in the hands of 0-6-0 'Jinty' No. 47279.

Vintage trains are not confined to Gala day running. On selected Sundays and Bank Holidays between May and August passengers are invited to travel the line 'as great grandad did!'

These Gala Weekends see all operable locomotives in action and Keighley is an ideal location to watch the comings and goings.

With a 1 in 58 gradient and a sharp right hand bend to contend with, departures can be spectacular, especially in late afternoon sunshine. During the February 2009 Gala B.R. Ivatt Class '2MT' 2-6-2 Side Tank No.41241 pilots W.D. 2-8-0 No. 90733 away from the station.

Earlier that month with snow covering the valley No. 41241 was working solo…

…creating a volcanic exhaust in in the frosty air as it worked its way up the hill.

Left:

Over the weekend 26 - 28 June 2009 the railway held its revamped Summer Gala which included vintage trains hauled by the Hudswell Clarke 0-6-0 tank 'Nunlow'. This locomotive was in ex. works condition having just emerged following restoration that had been carried out by its owners the 'Bahamas Locomotive Society' at their base alongside Ingrow Station.

Right:

Black Five No. 45212 plays to the photographer's gallery at the top of Keighley bank.

The Great Central Railway's LNER 2-8-0 Class 04 No. 63601 visited the line in the summer of 2009 and was photographed getting into its stride along the section of line known as 'Great Northern straight'.

The February 2008 Gala attracted two visiting locomotives. From the North Yorkshire Moors Railway came LNER K1 Class 2-6-0 No. 62005…

…whilst the Mid-Hants Railway provided their Ivatt 2-6-2T No. 41312. Both locomotives captured on the approach to Ingrow.

For the vintage trains on the 28 June 2009 'Nunlow' provided the motive power. (Photo Karl Heath)

Left:
The station building at Ingrow West was formerly the Midland Railway Station at Foulridge, Lancashire. It was dismantled, transported over the Pennines and rebuilt here, stone by stone!

Right:
A demonstration freight train, hauled by No. 62005 and banked by 'Jinty' No. 47279, makes its way up the valley.

Left:
At this point the railway leaves the industrial environment behind and the surrounding countryside takes on a more rural appearance. (Photo Karl Heath)

Right:
The vintage pairing of the 1887-built Lancashire and Yorkshire Railway's 0-6-0 No. 957 and the 1899-built Taff Vale Railway 0-6-2 Tank No. 85 make a stirring sight on the climb towards Damems.

On the 17 February 2008 No. 85 worked solo as it ran alongside the River Worth.

The October 2008 Gala saw the Churnet Valley Railway's S160 2-8-0 No. 5197 working services. The woods around Damems taking on an autumnal plume. (Photo Karl Heath)

Left:
Back in February 2008 the sun shone through the trees to illuminate No. 41312 piloting the railway's own Standard Tank No.80002.

Right:
957 is the one survivor of the Lancashire & Yorkshire Railway's Class 25 locomotives. They were better known as 'Ironclads' after the battleships of that name that were under construction when the first of the class were introduced in 1876.

The station at Damems is known as the smallest station in Britain, having a ticket-cum-station master's office, waiting room, signal box and station house. The signal man is notifying the footplate crew of the Keighley-bound train that there are passengers to pick up.

Left:
Having just passed over the Damems level crossing No. 63601 approaches the passing loop.

Right:
Great Western Railway No. 4953 'Pitchford Hall' is about to receive the token from the signalman and will soon be on its way with its obviously well packed train. This scene recorded during the February 2007 Gala.

Left:
No. 42729, the 'Jinty', climbs
Oakworth bank, a popular
location for photographers.
(Photo Karl Heath)

Right:
Lancashire & Yorkshire Railway
'Pug' No. 51218 is currently out
of service awaiting overhaul but
on 22 October 2000 it was in
full working order at the head of
an early morning freight.

33

Oakworth, the Railway Children station, is maintained in its Edwardian splendour being kept as near as possible in its 1905-1914 condition which includes gas lighting, classic enamel advertising signs and platform furniture of the period.

The oft used phrase 'Christmas card scene' seems most appropriate for this February 2009 view.

Left:
My favourite industrial locomotive is the former Haydock Foundry 0-6-0 Well Tank ' Bellerophon' which is owned by the Vintage Carriages Trust and currently based on the Foxfield Railway. I could not resist including this January 1999 shot of its departure from Oakworth in this album.

Right:
British Railways' Britannia Pacific No. 70013 'Oliver Cromwell' operated the last steam passenger train prior to the abolition of steam in 1968. It was restored to main line standard for the 40th anniversary of that last train and visited the KWVR for their February 2009 Gala.

WD No. 90733 powers its way round the curve on the approach to Mytholmes viaduct. This location offers the photographer the popular front three-quarter view and the equally impressive going-away shot.

(Photo Karl Heath)

The viaduct itself offers one of the best vistas on the railway. On 21 June 2009, in its last year of operation before expiry of its boiler certificate, No. 85 proudly passes by. (Photo Karl Heath)

True vintage! A Lancashire & Yorkshire locomotive hauling a train that includes two beautifully restored coaches originally owned by that same railway company.

June 2007 and the lush green landscape confirms that summer has arrived in the valley as No. 80002 glides towards Haworth.

Haworth Station retains its original form externally, but has been altered internally to provide a well stocked shop where the waiting room and ladies' room once stood.

The railway's locomotive works are housed in the former Midland Railway warehouse. The road bridge is a useful vantage point to see the locomotives prepared for their day's work.

If you don't fancy dodging the traffic on the bridge the signposted viewing and picnic area is a much safer location! (Photo Karl Heath)

October 2007 saw Great Western Railway 2-8-0 No. 3802 visiting the line from its normal base the Llangollen Railway.

No. 957 creates a near perfect exhaust trail in the cold autumnal air as it hauls its vintage stock away from Haworth.

After leaving Haworth the line is never far away from the course of Bridge House Beck...

...and again passes through stunning rural scenery.

Autumn tints encroach as 41241 passes through with a pick-up freight.

The bareness of winter allowing a clearer view of WD. No.90733 and its more substantial freight working.

The Santa Specials combine nostalgia and Christmas celebrations. (Photo Karl Heath)

Steam hauled trains, a frost encrusted landscape, clear blue skies and a nip in the air – what more could a railway photographer want for Christmas!

The 'top field' is the name photographers have given to this attractive location midway between Haworth and Oxenhope.

A perfect location to capture an entire vintage train in the frame.

Right:
Another 2009 vintage train, this time in the hands of the Taff Vale tank, storms through the tree-lined section beyond 'top field'.

LMS Jubilee '5XP' 4-6-0 No. 5690 'Leander' was a popular visitor to the Autumn Gala held over the weekend 13 to 15 October 2006.

Passing the same location on 13 February 2009 is No. 70013 'Oliver Cromwell'.

There are many footpaths along this stretch with a couple crossing over the railway. Clear instructions warn walkers to be on their guard.

On 2 August 2009
'Jinty' No. 47279 is
rounding the last curve
as it approaches
Oxenhope.

Oxenhope Station has always been the branch line's terminus and is this photographic journey's end.

In 2008 the Summer Steam Gala introduced a Main Line Steam Service between Keighley, Skipton and Hellifield. Such was its popularity that it seems set to become an annual event and in 2009 LMS 'Jubilee' Class 4-6-0 No.5690 'Leander' provided the motive power seen here thundering through Coniston Cold. (Photo Karl Heath)